Yard Sale

BY JAMES STEVENSON

GREENWILLOW BOOKS, NEW YORK

For Suçie

Watercolor paints and a black pen
were used for the full-color art.
The text type is Galliard BT.

First Edition
10 9 8 7 6 5 4 3 2 1

LIBRARY OF CONGRESS
CATALOGING-IN-PUBLICATION DATA

Stevenson, James (date)
Yard sale / by James Stevenson.
        p.   cm.
Summary: Simsbury is sitting under
his favorite tree when a red chair and
an accordion pass by, prompting him
to get up and take a look at the
Mud Flat Yard Sale.
ISBN 0-688-14126-9 (trade).
ISBN 0-688-14127-7 (lib. bdg.)
[1. Garage sales—Fiction.
2. Collectors and collecting—Fiction.
3. Humorous stories.]   I. Title.
PZ7.S84748Yar 1996   [Fic]—dc20
95-4445   CIP   AC

CONTENTS

1. Simsbury

Simsbury was sitting under his favorite tree when he saw a red chair go by.

Then he saw an accordion wriggling along behind the chair. It made weird wheezy sounds.

Simsbury got up to take a look.

Clifton and Rebecca were carrying the chair.

Margaret and Clyde were carrying the accordion.

Clyde put down his end of the accordion so
he could catch his breath.

"What's going on, Clyde?" called Simsbury.

"Hurry up, Clyde!" called Margaret. "You're
falling behind!"

Oliver was carrying
a pile of kitchen things.
"Where are you going?"
asked Simsbury.

"To the big . . ." said Oliver.

His pile began to wobble.

"To the big . . ."

His pile toppled,

and a pot fell on

Oliver's head.

"Yob sabe," said Oliver.

"What's a yob sabe?" said Simsbury.

Oliver took off the pot. "Yard sale," he said.

"What's a yard sale?" said Simsbury.

"It's where you take the stuff you don't want
anymore, and somebody else buys it," said
Oliver. "Everybody's going to the yard sale."

"I have stuff I don't want anymore," said
Simsbury. "Lots of it."

"Well, hurry home and get it," said Oliver.

"The yard sale is about to begin!"

The yard sale began at nine o'clock.
The first to arrive was Roy, with a couple of
picture frames. Arthur, Jackson, and Russell
were next. Arthur brought a cracked tea cup.
Jackson and Russell carried an old book.

Crocker arrived at nine-fifteen with an alarm
clock, two tattered neckties, and a broken
hockey stick.

"I don't believe anybody would want that
broken hockey stick," said Delphina.

"How do you know?" said Crocker. "It would
be perfect for a small hockey player."

Crocker put his things next to a lilac bush and looked around, rubbing his hands together. "Who wants the first chance to buy an alarm clock that is very rare and special?" he called.

"What's so rare and special about it?" asked Henry.

"The alarm is silent," said Crocker.

"Is that good?" said Henry.

"Of course it is!" said Crocker. "You don't want one of those nasty noisy alarms, do you? *Ring-Ring-Ring-Ring-Ring*!"

"No, I don't," said Henry. "I hate those."

"Then the silent alarm clock is the thing for you," said Crocker. "Fifty cents, please."

Henry looked at the clock. "Shouldn't it have hands?" he asked.

"Hands are extra," said Crocker. "You'd have to pay quite a bit more."

"Oh," said Henry. "How do you wind it? I don't see any key."

"This clock is pre-wound," said Crocker. "You'll never have to worry about winding it."

"Most clocks have lots of numbers on the front," said Henry. "Where are the other numbers?"

"Henry, Henry, Henry," said Crocker with a sigh. "Do you mean to tell me you don't remember where the numbers are on a clock?"

"Oh, no," said Henry. "I remember."

Henry gave Crocker fifty cents and took the clock.

"Don't show it to anybody," whispered Crocker.

"They might try to steal it."

Henry put the clock in his pocket and hurried
home, looking over his shoulder as he went.

"Who wants the first chance to buy a necktie once
worn by George Washington?" Crocker called.

3. Avery and Gail

Avery and Gail were watching the yard sale.

"I wish I had something to sell," said Avery,

"but I don't own anything."

"Neither do I," said Gail.

"Would you like to go smell the honeysuckle?"
  said Avery.

"Sure," said Gail.

"It will cost you three million dollars a sniff,"
  said Avery.

"That's a bargain," said Gail.

  They flew off to the honeysuckle together.

4. The Attic

Simsbury went up to his dusty attic. "This is where all the things I don't want to keep are kept," he said to himself. "Now's my chance to get rid of everything."

He pushed aside
the cobwebs and
began peering into
old boxes.
"My goodness,"
he said. "There's so
much I don't want."
He poked through
the piles. "Stuff and
more stuff," he said.

"Of course," said Simsbury, "there are a couple
of things I wouldn't want to sell, such as this
bicycle." He wiped away the dust. "Who knows
when I might want to go for a spin?"

He found a stack of picture postcards
and started to look at them.
"Lovely picture of a beach
at sunset," he said. "Better
hold on to that one. . . .
Oh, look at those
snowy mountains. . . ."

An hour later Simsbury had found his
old guitar and was sitting on a suitcase,
playing songs from long ago.

5. April's Comb

"This is a nice green comb, April," said Naomi.
"How much do you want for it?"

"Oh, I don't know if I can sell that green comb,"
said April. "It's very dear to me. It belonged to
my grandmother. She loved it. Then it belonged to
my mother. She loved it even more. It would
be very hard to let it go for any price."

"I'll give you fifteen cents," said Naomi.

"It's yours," said April.

6. The Footstool of Kings

"How much for that ratty-looking orange footstool?" said Matthew.

"That's a very old footstool," said Beth. "It came from a castle. Kings put their feet on it."

"How much?" said Matthew.

"Five cents," said Beth. "Not a penny less."

Matthew bought the orange footstool and
carried it away.

"Am I glad to get rid of that," said Beth.

"I never liked it the least bit."

Later Beth saw Matthew sitting under a tree
with his feet on the footstool.

"I love this footstool," said Matthew. "I don't
know how I ever lived without it."

All day long Beth thought about her old orange footstool. "How could Matthew like it?" she said to herself.

At the end of the day Beth went in search of Matthew.

She found Matthew by the river, sitting on the footstool. He was dozing.

"Matthew," said Beth. "Wake up!"

"My goodness," said Matthew. "I must have fallen asleep on my wonderful footstool."

"I want my footstool back," said Beth. "Here's your five cents."

"Ten cents," said Matthew. "Not a penny less."

"But you only paid five cents," said Beth.

"It's older now," said Matthew, "and more valuable."

"What?" said Beth.

"It came from a castle. . . ."

"It did not!" said Beth. She gave Matthew ten cents.

"Enjoy it," said Matthew.

Beth carried it away. "I'll be glad when this darn yard sale is over," she said to herself.

7. Delphina's Table

"ANYTHING ON THIS TABLE 5¢"

said a sign on Delphina's table. The table
was piled with all kinds of things.

Delphina was reading a magazine.

"I think I'll take this," said Leo.

"Just put a nickel in the jar," said Delphina.

Leo put a nickel in the jar.

A few moments later Delphina
stopped reading.

"Time for lunch," she said.

"Hey! Where's my peanut
butter sandwich?"

8. The Accordion

Margaret was showing the accordion to Nick.
"I can tell by looking at you that you like
beauty," said Margaret. "Am I right?"
"I guess I do," said Nick. "Sometimes."

"You enjoy beautiful music," said Margaret.

"If it's good," said Nick.

"Do you own an accordion?" asked Margaret.

"Not right now," said Nick. "No."

"If you owned one," said Margaret, "you could
  play beautiful music any time of day or night."

"I could?" said Nick.

"Under the stars," said Margaret. "By
  moonlight. When soft breezes blow . . ."

"How much would it cost?" said Nick.

"Fifty cents," said Margaret. "That's with
the strap."

"Okay," said Nick. He gave Margaret
the money.

"Hey, Clyde!" called Margaret. "I just sold
the accordion to Nick!"

"What?" said Clyde. "*I* just sold this end
to Myrna!"

"I want my money back!" said Myrna.

"I'm sorry," said Clyde, "but all sales are final."

"What do we do now?" said Nick.

"Share," said Margaret.

She and Clyde walked away quickly.

Nick and Myrna stared at each other across

the accordion.

9. Dusk

It was dusk when Simsbury arrived at the yard
sale. Only Beth was still there.

"I finally found something for the yard sale,"
said Simsbury. "My top hat."

"Too late," said Beth. "The yard sale is over."

"I missed it, eh?" said Simsbury.

"Yes, but you haven't missed the big party
down by the river," said Beth.

"Party?" said Simsbury.

"Music and dancing and plenty to eat,"
said Beth.

"It's lucky I didn't sell my hat," said Simsbury.

"Now I can wear it to the party."

10. The Party

At the party by the river there was lots of music and food. Myrna and Nick played their accordion together while people danced.

Crocker came to the party wearing one of his old neckties. When he saw Henry, he went over and gave Henry his fifty cents back.

"I've been thinking," said Crocker. "Your clock may need a few repairs."

"Thank you," said Henry. "But I like it anyway."

He gave Crocker twenty-five cents back.
Crocker gave Henry a necktie. "No charge," he said.

Matthew and Beth shared the orange
footstool while they ate ice cream and cake.
When the party was nearly over, Simsbury
played some old songs, and everybody sang.
Balloons drifted up across the moon.
As everyone walked home, they could hear
the strumming of the old guitar.